Land Speed Racing

by Steve Hendrickson

Consultant:
Hugh Fleming
Director, AMA Sports
American Motorcyclist Association

CAPSTONE BOOKS

an imprint of Capstone Press
Mankato, Minnesota

Capstone Books are published by Capstone Press
151 Good Counsel Drive, P.O. Box 669, Mankato, Minnesota 56002
http://www.capstone-press.com

Library of Congress Cataloging-in-Publication Data
Hendrickson, Steve.
    Land speed racing/by Steve Hendrickson.
    p. cm.—(Motorcycles)
    Includes bibliographical references (p. 45) and index.
    Summary: An introduction to motorcycle racing, describing its history,
development, equipment, and stars of the sport.
    ISBN 0-7368-0476-5
    1. Motorcycle racing—Juvenile literature. 2. Motorcycles, Racing—Juvenile
literature. [1. Motorcycle racing. 2. Motorcycles, Racing.] I. Title. II. Series.

GV1060 .H46 2000
796.7'5—dc21   99-055962

Editorial Credits
Blake Hoena, editor; Timothy Halldin, cover designer and illustrator; Heidi Schoof
    and Jodi Theisen, photo researchers

Photo Credits
Ben E. Wheeler, 34, 40
Don Vesco, 13, 21
Kenny Lyon, 30
Louise Ann Noeth, cover, 4, 8, 10, 16, 18, 22, 25, 28, 39, 44
Ron Cook, 6, 15, 26, 37

1 2 3 4 5 6 05 04 03 02 01 00

Table of Contents

Features

CHAPTER 1

Land Speed Racing

Land speed racing is a form of motorcycle and car racing. But land speed racers do not race against each other on racecourses. Instead, they try to set speed records on large, flat areas such as dry lake beds. Land speed racers race to see how fast their vehicles can go.

In 1909, William Cook set the earliest speed record for a motorcycle. He reached a speed of 75.9 miles (122.1 kilometers) per hour. He set this record at the Brooklands Racetrack in England.

Cook's speed record has been broken many times. Motorcycle manufacturers have designed better and faster motorcycles over the years. Currently, Dave Campos holds the world land

Land speed racers race to set speed records.

Racers put sponsors' names and logos on their motorcycles.

speed record for all types of motorcycles. In 1990, he set a record speed of 322.149 miles (518.434 kilometers) per hour while racing on a Harley-Davidson motorcycle. He achieved this at the Bonneville Salt Flats near Salt Lake City, Utah.

Goals of Land Speed Racing

Land speed racers receive few rewards for their efforts. Land speed competitions do not offer prize money to racers. Most land speed racers simply enjoy the sport's challenges. A land speed racer's goal is to set a new speed record. This is a difficult task.

Land speed racing has few sponsors. These companies provide motorcycles, motorcycle parts, and money to racers. Sponsors may be motorcycle manufacturers or companies that produce motorcycle parts and equipment. These companies place their names and logos on the motorcycles of the racers they sponsor. But most land speed racers have to pay for their own racing and equipment costs.

Motorcycle manufacturers sometimes hire racers to race their motorcycles. These manufacturers hope their motorcycles might set a land speed record. Customers will then see how well the manufacturer's motorcycles perform. These people may decide to buy one of the manufacturer's motorcycles because of its racing performance.

Land Speed Racing Associations
The Southern California Timing Association (SCTA) was formed in 1938. The SCTA is a

group of land speed racing clubs in southern California. Racers must be a member of one of these clubs to race in SCTA events. During the summer, the SCTA holds monthly races.

The Utah Salt Flats Racing Association (USFRA) was established in 1976. The USFRA helps organize the World of Speed week at the Bonneville Salt Flats. Racers must be a member of the USFRA to race during this event. The USFRA also attempts to preserve the salt flats for future racing events.

The East Coast Timing Association (ECTA) was established in 1994. This organization provides racers with a land speed racing track in the eastern United States. These racers compete on a runway at Maxton Army Air Base in North Carolina.

Land speed racing associations organize racing events.

CHAPTER 2

Land Speed Basics

Early land speed racers attempted to set speed records on racetracks and flat, sandy beaches. But most racetracks do not have long, straight stretches of road. Land speed racers need these for their vehicles to reach high speeds. Hard surfaces also are better for racing than beaches. In the 1930s, many racers raced on dry lake beds in southern California's deserts. Since 1948, most land speed racing records have been set at the Bonneville Salt Flats.

The Bonneville Salt Flats

The Bonneville Salt Flats are the remains of a huge salt lake. This area once was covered by saltwater similar to ocean water. The salt

Land speed racers have raced on the Bonneville Salt Flats since 1948.

remained after the lake's water dried up. This salt then formed a hard, thick crust. The surface of the salt flats is large and flat. The salt flats cover more than 44,000 acres (18,000 hectares) of land.

Land speed racing events are held at the Bonneville Salt Flats a few times each year. The Southern California Timing Association holds its Speed Week there every August. The Utah Salt Flats Racing Association also holds events there.

Before a race, officials prepare two tracks on the salt flats. One track is longer than the other. The longer track may be 5 miles (8 kilometers) in length or longer. Vehicles that can reach speeds greater than 175 miles (282 kilometers) per hour race on this track. The shorter track may be as long as 3 miles (5 kilometers). It is used for vehicles that race slower than 175 miles (282 kilometers) per hour.

Officials drag a sled across the surface of each track to make it smooth. They then paint a long, straight black line on the salt's white surface. Officials set up large signboards at

Race officials set up timers on land speed tracks to record racers' speeds.

each mile (1.6 kilometers) along the tracks. Racers use these signs to know where they are on the tracks. Officials also set up electronic timers at each mile to record racers' speeds.

El Mirage

Outside Utah, only a few other places exist that are suitable for land speed racing. The most well known of these is El Mirage in southern California. Land speed racers have raced on El Mirage since the 1930s.

El Mirage is a shallow lake in the winter. During the spring, the desert heat dries up the water. The lake bed then becomes a hard, flat surface of dried mud.

The racing area at El Mirage is not as large as the Bonneville Salt Flats' racing area. The 1999 track at El Mirage was only 1.3 miles (2.1 kilometers) long. Racers cannot race as fast at El Mirage as they can at the Bonneville Salt Flats. The fastest motorcycle speed records at El Mirage are slightly more than 200 miles (322 kilometers) per hour.

The cars and motorcycles racing at El Mirage may tear up the mud surface. The tracks then need to be moved to another section of the lake bed.

Maxton Army Air Base

The Bonneville Salt Flats and El Mirage are far from racers who live in the eastern United States and Canada. Because of this, racers in North Carolina formed the East Coast Timing

During the summer, land speed racers compete on El Mirage's dried lake bed.

Association. The ECTA's goal was to find a place for land speed racing on the east coast.

The U.S. government built the Maxton Army Air Base in 1942. It was a training base for pilots learning to fly gliders. Pilots use air currents to fly these lightweight aircraft. Gliders are not powered by engines.

The Maxton Air Base has three runways. But only two of them are used by the military today.

Racers must first make a qualifying run before they can try to set a new land speed record.

The third runway was covered in dirt, weeds, and trees. ECTA members cleaned up this runway. They then repaired the runway and turned it into a racing surface. This surface is 1.9 miles (3.1 kilometers) long. The track is long enough for vehicles to reach speeds of more than 200 miles (322 kilometers) per hour.

Salt Flat Racing in Australia

Land speed racing also takes place in Australia. One of the largest salt flats is Lake Gairdner. It is in southern Australia.

Lake Gairdner is much larger than the Bonneville Salt Flats. Lake Gairdner's surface also is much thicker and harder. Tent stakes cannot be pounded into its surface. Vehicles are easier to drive at high speeds over hard surfaces.

Lake Gairdner is in a remote area. No cities are located near it. Racers camp near the salt flats at night.

The Australian government protects Lake Gairdner. All vehicles that travel on the salt flats must first be washed. This prevents vehicles from tracking dirt onto the salt flats.

Setting a New Speed Record

It is difficult to set a new land speed record. First, racers must qualify by reaching a speed at least .001 miles (.0016 kilometers) per hour faster than the existing record. Racers need to qualify to prove that they may be able to break the existing land speed record. After qualifying, a racer must make a second run to set a new speed record. During these two runs, the racer's average speed must be greater than the record

Aerodynamically-designed motorcycles have smooth body panels.

speed. The racer then may have set a new record with the average speed.

Race officials must inspect the racer's motorcycle before the record is awarded. Officials make sure the motorcycle meets safety rules. They also make sure the motorcycle meets all the rules for the class in which it is raced. The racer has officially set a new record if the motorcycle passes this inspection.

Wind Resistance

A great deal of power is needed to push a motorcycle through the air. Wind resistance is greater at higher speeds. This air force opposes movement. In land speed racing, motorcycles must cut through the air with little resistance to reach high speeds.

Land speed racers reduce wind resistance by streamlining their motorcycles. This can be done by decreasing the size of their motorcycle's front end. Motorcycles then have a smaller area that pushes against the force of the air.

An aerodynamic design also can lessen wind resistance. Aerodynamically-designed motorcycles have features that allow the air to flow smoothly around and past the motorcycle. These motorcycles have smooth body panels with no bumps or gaps. They also may have a pointed front end.

Don Vesco

Currently, Don Vesco holds more than 20 car and motorcycle land speed records. He has recorded the fastest speed for a motorcycle at 333.117 miles (536.085 kilometers) per hour. He also has recorded the fastest time for a wheel-driven vehicle at 438.897 miles (706.317 kilometers) per hour. The engines in wheel-driven vehicles apply power directly to the wheels to make them turn. Most cars are wheel-driven vehicles.

1999 – Set a wheel-driven land speed record of 427.832 miles (688.510 kilometers) per hour.

1997 – Recorded the fastest wheel-driven vehicle time. But he was unable to complete a second run to set a record.

1978 – Recorded the fastest motorcycle time. But a bad tire caused him to stop before setting a land speed record.

1978 – Set a motorcycle land speed record of 318.598 miles (512.720 kilometers) per hour at Bonneville.

1975 – Became the first motorcyclist to reach a speed of more than 300 miles (480 kilometers) per hour. He set a record speed of 303.812 miles (488.925 kilometers) per hour at Bonneville.

1970 – Became the first person to race a motorcycle at more than 250 miles (400 kilometers) per hour. He set a record speed of 251.924 miles (405.421 kilometers) per hour at Bonneville.

1955 – Raced a motorcycle for the first time at the Bonneville Salt Flats at age 16.

CHAPTER 3

Motorcycles and Racing Classes

Almost any type of motorcycle can be used for land speed racing. Most beginning racers race stock motorcycles. These motorcycles have no special equipment. Few changes have been made to them. They are similar to motorcycles sold at motorcycle dealerships. This helps make land speed racing more affordable than other kinds of racing. No expensive changes are needed to prepare a stock motorcycle for land speed racing.

More experienced land speed racers often race specially designed motorcycles. These motorcycles may have streamlined bodies. They

Experienced land speed racers often race specially designed motorcycles.

also may have specially designed engines. Some of the fastest motorcycles can reach speeds of more than 300 miles (480 kilometers) per hour.

Motorcycle Classes

Land speed racers may race in several classes. A motorcycle's class depends on its engine size, frame type, engine type, and the fuel it burns. It may even depend on how old the motorcycle is. Each racing class has its own land speed record.

A series of letters and numbers tells what class a motorcycle is in. The first letter or letters tell what type of frame a motorcycle has. The next letter or letters identify the type of engine and fuel a motorcycle uses. The number that follows these letters represents a motorcycle's engine size. For example, Dave Campos set the fastest motorcycle land speed record with an S-F 3000 cubic centimeter (cc) class motorcycle. His motorcycle had an S class frame and an F class engine. Its engine size was 3000cc.

Frames

There are four main types of motorcycle frames in land speed racing. Each is identified by a letter.

Rick Yacoucci holds the fastest land speed record for all P class motorcycles.

Production (P) class motorcycles have no special equipment. They also are called stock motorcycles. Racers can change only a few things on these motorcycles. These changes may include adding tires designed for racing. Rick Yacoucci holds the fastest land speed record for all P class motorcycles. In 1999, he

Special construction motorcycles do not look like standard motorcycles.

set a record of 201.708 miles (324.609 kilometers) per hour.

Land speed racers may make more changes to modified (M) class motorcycles. These changes may include making the motorcycles' frames stronger. This makes motorcycles more stable at high speeds. But class rules state that the shape of the frame must remain the same. The tires and handlebars also can be changed. Racers can remove lights, turn signals, and gauges to make their motorcycles lighter. Gauges measure a motorcycle's speed, fuel, and oil. Dave Matson holds the fastest land speed record for all M class motorcycles. In 1988, he set a record speed of 210.357 miles (338.528 kilometers) per hour while riding a Vincent motorcycle.

Special construction (A) class motorcycles do not look like standard motorcycles. They may have custom-built frames and special bodywork to improve aerodynamics. Racers may change the shape of the frame on these motorcycles. They may make them longer or closer to the ground. This helps decrease wind resistance. But the bodywork on the motorcycle has to remain open. It cannot enclose the racer. Les Ranger holds the fastest land speed record for all A class motorcycles. In 1991, he set a record speed of 219.339 miles (352.982 kilometers) per hour racing a Honda motorcycle.

The fastest motorcycles are in the streamliner (S) class. These motorcycles have long, narrow

Streamliners have cockpits in which racers sit.

custom-built frames. Streamliners' bodies also are fully enclosed. Racers sit in a covered cockpit. Because of this, streamliner racers cannot use their legs to hold their motorcycle upright when it is stopped. Small skis mounted on the motorcycle's sides hold it upright when stopped and at low speeds. At high speeds, the skis are raised off the ground. Streamliners can have one or more engines. Some streamliners even use car engines to power them. Dave Campos holds the fastest land speed record for all S class motorcycles.

Engine Classes

Land speed racers can use several types of engines for their motorcycles. Engine types are divided into three main classes.

Production (P) class engines use gasoline. These engines also have not been modified in any way.

Modified-gasoline (G) class engines use gasoline for fuel. But modifications can be made to these engines. These changes help produce more power. They may include changing the engine to burn more gasoline during each engine cycle. Don Vesco holds the fastest land speed record for all G class engines. In 1975, he set a record speed of 303.812 miles (488.925 kilometers) per hour. He set this record while racing an S-G class motorcycle.

Modified-fuel (F) class engines use fuels other than gasoline. These fuels include alcohol, nitromethane, and nitrous oxide. Nitromethane

Fuel is burned inside an engine's cylinders to create power.

also is used to power rockets. Some racers mix these fuels with gasoline. Chemical fuels mixed with gasoline create more power when burned than gasoline alone.

Engine Sizes

An engine's size indicates the size of its cylinders. A cylinder is the space inside an engine where fuel is burned to create power.

There are many classes for engine size. Production and modified class motorcycle engine sizes can range from 50cc to 2000cc. Special construction and streamliner class motorcycles can have engine sizes from 50cc to more than 3000cc.

Larger engines often are more powerful than smaller engines. Motorcycles with larger engines then can reach higher speeds than motorcycles with smaller engines. The land speed record for an A-G 100cc class motorcycle is 93.760 miles (150.888 kilometers) per hour. The land speed record for an A-G 3000cc class motorcycle is 200.022 miles (321.895 kilometers) per hour.

Bonneville Records

Class	Racer	Year	Record
50cc:			
P-P	Teresa Wagner	1995	73.419 mph (118.153 km/h)
M-F	Jim Ahrens	1979	81.314 mph (130.859 km/h)
A-G	Jim Ahrens	1979	78.190 mph (125.831 km/h)
100cc:			
P-P	Teresa Wagner	1998	78.051 mph (125.607 km/h)
M-G	Belen Wagner	1988	95.706 mph (154.020 km/h)
A-G	Belen Wagner	1991	93.760 mph (150.888 km/h)
S-G	Rick Vesco	1968	113.249 mph (182.252 km/h)
250cc:			
P-P	M. Gassaway	1989	129.874 mph (209.006 km/h)
M-G	Mike Burns	1995	137.169 mph (220.746 km/h)
A-G	Harry Fair	1978	133.002 mph (214.040 km/h)
S-F	Don Vesco	1973	202.445 mph (325.795 km/h)
500cc:			
P-P	Shane Kenneally	1998	148.242 mph (238.566 km/h)
M-G	Scott Guthrie	1988	168.309 mph (270.860 km/h)
A-F	Scott Guthrie	1988	170.833 mph (274.922 km/h)
S-F	J. Thomas	1958	212.288 mph (341.635 km/h)
750cc:			
M-F	J. Long	1990	167.076 mph (268.875 km/h)
A-F	Scott Guthrie	1990	167.824 mph (270.079 km/h)
S-G	Don Vesco	1970	251.924 mph (405.421 km/h)

Class	Racer	Year	Record

1000cc:

Class	Racer	Year	Record
P-P	Jason McVicar	1999	178.667 mph (287.529 km/h)
M-F	Ron Cook	1997	173.048 mph (278.486 km/h)
A-G	Jason McVicar	1999	169.845 mph (273.332 km/h)
A-F	Ron Cook	1997	172.091 mph (276.946 km/h)
S-F	B. Munro	1967	183.586 mph (295.445 km/h)

1350cc:

Class	Racer	Year	Record
P-P	Rick Yacoucci	1999	201.708 mph (324.609 km/h)
M-G	Ron Cook	1997	178.879 mph (287.870 km/h)
A-BG	Les Ranger	1991	219.339 mph (352.982 km/h)
S-G	Sam Wheeler	1996	285.747 mph (459.853 km/h)
S-F	Sam Wheeler	1999	294.855 mph (474.510 km/h)

2000cc:

Class	Racer	Year	Record
M-G	S & S Cycle	1995	166.053 mph (267.229 km/h)
M-F	Dave Matson	1988	210.357 mph (338.528 km/h)
A-G	Dan Kinsey	1984	171.410 mph (275.850 km/h)
A-F	J. Angerer	1973	201.432 mph (324.165 km/h)
S-G	Don Vesco	1975	303.812 mph (488.925 km/h)
S-F	C. Rayborn	1970	265.492 mph (427.256 km/h)

3000cc:

Class	Racer	Year	Record
A-G	Tom Elrod	1979	200.022 mph (321.895 km/h)
A-F	Tom Elrod	1981	196.957 mph (316.963 km/h)
S-G	Tom Elrod	1974	197.047 mph (317.108 km/h)
S-F	Dave Campos	1990	322.149 mph (518.434 km/h)

CHAPTER 4

Racing Skills
and Safety

Land speed racing can be a dangerous sport. Safety is very important when racing at high speeds. Racers must meet certain qualifications to race. Racers must be at least 16 years old and have a driver's license. Racers then must be licensed to land speed race.

To become licensed, racers first make a test run at less than 124 miles (200 kilometers) per hour. Successful racers then receive a class E competition license for land speed racing.

A rider can earn a higher class license by making safe runs at faster speeds. But land speed racers are not allowed to race at speeds

Safety is important to land speed racers.

faster than is permitted by their license. Racers with a class D license can race at speeds as fast as 149 miles (240 kilometers) per hour. Class C racers can race as fast as 174 miles (280 kilometers) per hour. Class B racers can race at speeds as fast as 199 miles (320 kilometers) per hour. Racers with a class A license are allowed to race at more than 200 miles (322 kilometers) per hour.

Racers cannot advance more than one class at a time. They must get a class E license before they can receive a class D license. Racers can be suspended for racing faster than their license allows. They then will not be allowed to land speed race.

Safety Clothing

Racers must wear clothing that helps protect them while racing. To race, a racer must have a full-face helmet and a one-piece leather riding suit. Racers also need leather gloves and boots for protection.

Streamliner racers also must wear a fireproof suit. These racers sit in an enclosed cockpit. During crashes, they may not be able to easily

Motorcycle accidents at high speeds can be very serious.

get out of the cockpit. A fireproof suit helps protect racers if their motorcycle catches on fire.

Safety First

Motorcycles can be dangerous even at standard highway speeds. Safety is even more important in land speed racing. Motorcycle crashes at speeds of 200 miles (322 kilometers) per hour can seriously injure or kill racers.

Race organizers consider three elements to help keep land speed racing safe. These include the racer, the motorcycle, and the racecourse. They establish rules that apply to each of these elements.

All racers are licensed. This helps officials make sure that all racers can handle the high speeds of land speed racing. Racers who break the rules or ride dangerously can be disqualified. Racers also must wear proper safety equipment such as helmets, gloves, and boots. This equipment must meet safety guidelines set by racing associations.

Race officials also carefully examine the motorcycles. Officials inspect each motorcycle to make sure it is built and maintained safely. Racing organizations such as the SCTA have strict rules regarding how a motorcycle can be built or modified.

The safety rules also require racers to have special equipment on some motorcycles. Faster motorcycles need special racing tires. These tires are specially designed for use at high

Land speed racers wear helmets and leather suits to protect themselves.

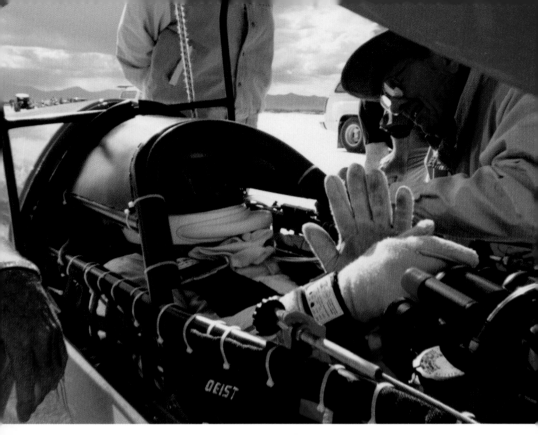

Racers need special safety equipment for streamliners.

speeds. Streamliner class motorcycles must have special equipment to protect racers. The enclosed cockpits must have a fire extinguisher system. This system helps put out any fires that may start during a race or crash. Streamliners must have latches that allow racers to easily open the cockpit. Racers also must wear a special racing harness. These straps are similar to seat belts. They hold racers in place.

The racecourse also must be safe. Officials patrol the course to make sure it is clear of debris. Sharp objects on the course could pop a tire and cause an accident. Officials also make sure no vehicles cross the racecourse. A collision at racing speeds would be very dangerous. Fire trucks and ambulance crews are ready to help during accidents. Race officials communicate by radio. Officials watch the racers carefully so they can radio for help if there is an accident.

Race officials work hard to make sure land speed racing is safe for all racers. Racers then can safely enjoy the challenges and excitement of land speed racing.

Words to Know

aerodynamic (air-oh-dye-NAM-mik)—designed to cut through the air with little resistance

cockpit (KOK-pit)—the area where racers sit in a streamliner motorcycle

cylinder (SIL-uhn-dur)—the space in an engine where fuel is burned to create power

gauge (GAYJ)—an instrument used for measuring; a motorcycle's gauges may measure the amount of fuel in a motorcycle's gas tank.

glider (GLYE-dur)—a lightweight aircraft that is flown by using air currents

modify (MOD-uh-fye)—to change

nitromethane (nye-troh-MEH-thane)—a fuel used to power rockets; nitromethane also can be mixed with gasoline to power motorcycles for land speed racing.

salt flats (SAWLT FLATSS)—areas of land that were once covered by saltwater; a hard, thick crust of salt formed after the water dried up.

saltwater (SAWLT-wah-tur)—water that is salty; saltwater is found in oceans.

sponsor (SPON-sur)—a company that may provide a land speed racer with a motorcycle, equipment, or money to race

stock motorcycle (STOK MOH-tur-sye-kuhl)—a motorcycle with no special equipment

streamliner (STREEM-line-uhr)—a motorcycle designed to cut through the wind with little resistance

wind resistance (WIND ri-ZISS-tuhnss)—an air force that opposes the motion of an object; wind resistance increases as an object's speed increases.

To Learn More

Dregni, Michael. *Motorcycle Racing.*
MotorSports. Mankato, Minn.: Capstone
Books, 1994.

Noeth, Louise Ann. *Bonneville Salt Flats.*
Osceola, Wis.: MBI Publishing, 1999.

Otfinoski, Steven. *Wild on Wheels:*
Motorcycles Then and Now. Here We Go!
New York: Marshall Cavendish, 1998.

Schleifer, Jay. *Bonneville!: Quest for the Land*
Speed Record. Out to Win. Parsippany, N.J.:
Crestwood House, 1995.

Useful Addresses

American Motorcyclist Association
13515 Yarmouth Drive
Pickerington, OH 43147

Canadian Motorcycle Association
P.O. Box 448
Hamilton, ON L8L 1J4
Canada

East Coast Timing Association
44 Ravenwood Drive
Fletcher, NC 28732

Southern California Timing Association
2517 Sycamore Drive # 353
Simi Valley, CA 93065

Utah Salt Flats Racing Association
P.O. Box 27365
Salt Lake City, UT 84127-0365

Internet Sites

American Motorcyclist Association
http://www.ama-cycle.org

Canadian Motorcycle Association
http://www.canmocycle.ca

Southern California Timing Association
http://www.scta-bni.org

Utah Salt Flats Racing Association
http://www.saltflats.com

Index